Walking Lorton Bluff

poems by

Paul Stroble

Finishing Line Press
Georgetown, Kentucky

Walking Lorton Bluff

ABOUT THE AUTHOR

Paul Stroble has four other Finishing Line Press books: *Dreaming at the Electric Hobo* (2015), *Little River* (2017), *Small Corner of the Stars* (2017), and *Backyard Darwin* (2019).

One of his poems, "Stereoscope," won first place in the Kentucky State Poetry Society's adult contest in 2016.

Another of his poems, "Cassettes," won Arts in Transit's 2019 MetroLines poetry contest, among fifteen other winners.

Walking Lorton Bluff includes a poem, "Land of Lincoln," that was published in Paddock Review and was nominated for a Pushcart Prize.

Paul has also written religious curriculum like *What Do Other Faiths Believe?* (Abingdon Press, 2003), *You Gave Me a Wide Place: Holy Places of Our Lives* (2006), and *What About Religion and Science?* (Abingdon Press, 2007).

Publisher: Leah Maines
Editor: Christen Kincaid
Cover Art: Paul Stroble
Author Photo: Jeannie Liautaud Photography
Cover Design: Elizabeth Maines McCleavy

Order online: www.finishinglinepress.com
also available on amazon.com

Author inquiries and mail orders:
Finishing Line Press
P. O. Box 1626
Georgetown, Kentucky 40324
U. S. A.

Table of Contents

1 This Side of Epochs 1

2 April 12, 1859 19

3 Correlations 31

4 A Parting Kiss 47

Notes 57

Wherever men and women are persecuted ... that place must—at that moment—become the center of the universe.

Elie Wiesel

My South Carolina ancestors James Starrett Carson (c. 1762-1835), a Revolutionary War veteran, and his wife Elizabeth West (c. 1760-1835) were early settlers of Fayette County, Illinois, where I was born and raised.

Their son, John Carson (1794-1844), married Margaret Parkinson (1799-1870).

*John and Margaret's son, **James P. Carson** (1819-1859), married **Permelia Swanson** (dates not known).*

James and Permelia's son, Wesley M. (Mac) Carson (1855-1924), was my dad's maternal grandfather.

Recently I returned to the country cemetery where John and James P. are buried, overlooking the Kaskaskia (Okaw) River.

These poems are to be read in sequence, as my thoughts drifted among moments historical and personal while I walked among the graves.

I

This Side of Epochs

Quiet for daydreams,
            I drive to the bluff and park
where the road slopes
            to the cultivated floodplain.
The combine driver passes, and we wave,
            good neighbors for the day.

Oaks lean toward the Okaw
            as if to gain a closer view
of folks who cast fishing lines
            into the lively water as it flows southwest.

Clouds and contrails drift,
            droplets around dust
in cool upper air.

A child thinks: *God shapes clouds,
            the ice cream cone,
the rabbit, and the leaf.*

We float with currents, we change,
            we are dust.
                        Are we clouds?

Beneath casket spray grass,
                    graves lie regular
with room for more.

I read names of kinfolk known in eureka moments:
                    the wife, the child listed in one census
but not the next, a noticed date,
                    lives ephemeral as wind.

Across the northward fence,
                    a farmhouse day begins:
doors close, engines start,
                    the radio sings…

                    Here he is:
Toward the bluff's far side,
                    my ancestor's stone is clear:

James P. Carson
Died April 12, 1859
Aged 39 ys 5 ms 14 ds

A carved hand points upward,
                    mild promise of Heaven.

He was shot and killed by another hunter
mistaking his call for that of a turkey,
                    reads the county history,
and my great-aunt told me
                    as she'd heard, *Poor Papa,*
scarcely four years old,
he hardly knew his father.
                    The friend knew he'd made a horrible mistake
as soon as he shot.

But that day started as any other,
                    perhaps with a kiss from his young wife
as he went out the door.

Driving here, I passed crop rows
       strolling toward timber,
round bales that seem to grow,

          and pumpjack wells:
steel grasshoppers
      rocking up and down,

with each stroke twenty liters of oil
          drawn from sandstone pools
of Pennsylvanian age
      along anticlines of this Illinois basin—

though not for us, our family farms.
      1940s test wells on the back eighty
produced nothing,

          consequence of land claims
five generations ago
      for rich soil and timber beauty
as my kinfolk spent their days

plowing, harvesting,
trading in town…
        and for me,
as Thoreau could say, beloved lands

explored and tapped for words
      while the oil man thinks
he's the richer man.

Once, glaciers drained and formed valleys
                for these Pleistocene hills,

fields became tides
                of an inland sea,
the waves were prairie grass,
                wild and hard to turn with the plow.

                        Peninsulas were sycamore and oak
where you might lose your way
                and, dying, reach for God's blood
on pedals of dogwood.

Nothing is more yielding than water,
                reads the *Dao De Jing,*
but for moving the strong, nothing is better—

including ice that creates topography
                and, indirectly, souls.

I warm my soul today
this side of epochs.

Confederation of the great Miami,
        Illini home;

      My ancestors told of a man
who rode into town, circa 1845,
        and recalled his people, camps, villages,
mounds from years before,

      even then a time when few whites
had ever seen a Native man,
        knowing only the trace of his stories.

      Hunt for arrowheads
in these bottoms and find perhaps
        a Hopewell point,
light tan chert and thin,
        needle tip still sharp,

         fallen into prairie grass
when the animal was carried to camp,
        long before tribes ceded lands to whites,

Native families moving, families gone, killed…

scanning land at your feet
        to glimpse the sacred thing,
                a hunt's sharp memory.

I drove here by U.S. 51
        and saw Lincoln's homely profile
on signs of his Heritage Trail,

        Land of Lincoln license plates
up and down my childhood two-lane

        where grain elevators stand
along the Sixth Circuit;
        filling station postcards four score and seven;

                crabapple trees on old farms,
motels, garages, parks,
corndogs on Route 66.

        We trim the honeysuckle
from the old picnic place on 51
and have our food by the tangled bank.

Is it too much to say
that stones themselves cry out
        with malice toward none?

Abe and Jesus vie for which
we Illinois folks heard first,
                saving souls or saving the Union,
        crossing the Jordan or the Sangamon.

Once, we paused with our sodas
        at the end of the road down the hill
by the Okaw's banks.

        I thought: Shiva pushed the channels
and from the god's hair, rushing water;

        Sarasvati, meandering, disappearing,
first river and her blessed song;

        The God of Israel, whose prophet Amos calls up
the mighty river of justice,
whose chariots and throne are aflame,
        Elisha calling, *My father, my father!*

Countryside baptizes stories,
        pioneer cabins in boundaries of timber,
                pioneer flatboats, pay 20 cents a bushel.
        Waters of justice, creek waters of memory.

I watch the Okaw below,
                knowing how broken tree limbs rush
toward the great channel first seen
        by Marquette who, fearful of being forgotten,
asked that his grave be marked
                with a cross

Wishful thinking: a train's
lonesome call.

In the late frontier days,
          iron roads promised
Illinois destiny.

                    Tracks were laid
beside the wagon roads.
          Locomotives burned cord wood
then Illinois coal, carried cargo
                    that brought no agony
or excuses that you didn't know.

                    Family men put in the standard gauge line
for the Nickel Plate Line toward East St. Louis
and once there drank in the clubs
                    with the meatpackers off their shifts.

Now, walk the tracks with your music
          or your gun and never fear missing
a whistle's warning, rain or shine.

I daydream that I start West,
                    hike night and day

till I reach the Mississippi
          and hear the beat of trains on the MacArthur Bridge
like East St. Louis jazz.

Did you love a hobby when you were young?
Once, my John Carson family notes
    were spread out my bed with my rock LPs
and my buddy said, no great shock,
        Heeeeere's Johnny!...

    I was a long-haired teen with a clipboard,
searching for ancestor graves
among the grass cool where I walked,

    those summer days with my '63 Chevy
passed on to me from Grandma:

stick-shift, AM adequate, a dogeared
        Spoon River Anthology on the seat
and cool air provided by the hole
in the floorboard,
      near Flintstone quality

      for a historian's bare feet.

John's son was James P.
        and John's father was James—

James Starrett Carson,
        veteran of the Battle of King's Mountain,
perhaps kin to Kit Carson
                though no proof exists.

        President Monroe signed for James
                a land grant
and the days' joys were jasmine and magnolia,
        live oak and hanging Spanish moss
by the Saluda River

until he and his family left those behind,
                went West
                        and settled this county in Jackson's time.

I dream the way this place might have looked then,
        old trees, grass that grew above a person's head
and might go to flames like nothing.

                The same sun that burned the skin of ancestors
rises above the dark timber,
the same stars concealed in day
        made paths for runaway slaves
for their own liberty.

                I remember when local folks
honored the Revolutionary soldiers with fireworks
shouted at the football field
                and at the lake, with proud colors
of red, white, and blue on our small streets

        as neighbors lit bottle rockets
and families shared and children laughed,
free in a free land.

The air is fresh, the birds call,
doves mourn.

Blooms of wild dill at the timber's edge,
        red berries of bush honeysuckle,
mulberry and button bush
with autumn olive.

                A bur oak's branches lie low enough
to smack a daydreaming walker
        (this happened to a friend…)
and inspire with its gnarled expanse.

Back home are my botany books
        by Darwin, Hooker, Humboldt,
Asa Gray whose Schoolbook
        is beauty in lists:

pesorlea of Illinois prairies,
hoary when young,
its flowers in short penciled racemes,

gladiolas the corn-flag,
short filaments like those of the Levant,
scarlet leaves like those of the Cape.

        I take ribbons
from the pages of explorers
and tie bouquets of Earth's flowers,
        then place them at kinfolk stones.

If I could paint in Hudson River style
all my childhood's hills,
the flowers, fields, and butterflies,

I'd do nothing else
but render landscapes as iconography
until I ask once more for mercy
and go among graves till Heaven,

while my carved name remains
on oil paintings of tree trunks,
and folks would depart in tears
from the beauty I rendered.

Yet, all good things…
Men in hats and women in parasols,
horses and wagons and birds about the sky
live in bright mid-century landscapes,

but those artists painted scenes
in two versions, blessedness and sin,
so by the time of war, all the people
have taken sides, and the hills are shadowed.

Permelia, my distant mother,
I know when landscape darkens
with no change of tone,

when grief turns the brightest hue a horror,
familiar scenes sicken
with what might have been
and time is hollowed out,

until beauty finally gladdens
and God pulls comfort from the black.

I choose flowers
for your unknown grave.

During a season of friendship
                    I liked to shoot
and learned the way time sharpens,
                    that emptying focus and burst
of satisfaction at a true aim:
          a pastime to which I might return
if a friend lends me

          any good choice of gun depending
on the game, the feel and ease of operation.
                    A friend uses a Benelli Black Eagle
that comes in a model for lefties like her.

          Dad had his Browning.
He served up rabbit, deer, and squirrel.
They're good eating! Just like chicken!
          I swear he said that.

          Once, each town had a slaughterhouse
near the daily goings-on
if you didn't do the task yourself.
          Ancient priests knew, too,
where to draw the knife

          through joints with ease,
and sacred towns
          saved aromas of roasting meat
for Ares, Artemus,
                    and in Holy Land, the Lord.

My meat is supermarket,

          but for clay pigeons,
                    I'm your huckleberry.

Never spin your pistol
        like they do in shows.
Spin your empty cup instead
and you won't risk a wound, a life.
                Any good hunter will scold you to be careful.

        It's almost too much to bear
that Dad's uncle, James T. Carson,
        slipped in his boat
and his gun went off into himself
and there was nothing anyone could do,

1909 and another James is gone,
        grandfather, grandson.

Why, O Lord,
do you stand far off?
Why do you hide yourself
in times of trouble?

The Lord is your keeper,
the Lord is your shade at your right hand,
the Lord will keep you from all evil,
the Lord will keep your life.

Where is God, when the harming chariots
ride hard?

Where is God
in the far country
        of our muddy boots?

L'homme armé doibt on doubter,
"The armed man should be feared":
        God's bold servant the archangel Michael
assists our souls at death's time.

        Here on the bluff
are men disarmed and carried
beyond the Jordan.

Here is a Lorton,
        cousin to the Carsons;

others whose lives are summed up
by companies and regiments.

Remember when we visited Fort Sumter:
        with our bonnie friend;
        as the plaques teach,
two years to the day
                after James P. died,
April 12, 1861;

and in the hearts of people
        prayers went up for war,
                or prayers for peace,
                        for a swift end,

till the thousands fell,
debt paid for the blood of the lash,

fire and wind and some voice of God—

—a sudden, gentle sound,

a vole?

wee beastie?

Grass where civilians, soldiers go
        is what it knows
while folk like me live and work,
        go oft astray,
and walk in quiet places.

2

April 12, 1859

Coincidences of history
                crisscross in daydreams
        for my graveyard stroll.

That day is John Brown
in the times of great slave auctions
        and laws pressing fugitive slaves
who are dashing North—

his second day in Petersboro
with his *Secret Six,* speaking, gaining funds.

If I were to point out
the man in all this world,
I think most truly Christian, writes his friend,
I would point to John Brown.

He'll be hanged by year's end, but
                his great cause is sworn and sealed.

Those who teach of Time,
        Charles and Mary Lyell were that day
on the sands over which the waves
were rolling on a very bright day,
the Rhine at low tide,
sluices made by Napoleon I,

and hills where we gathered wild pansy,
a small Myosotis, Stellaria, groundsel,
large patches of brilliant tulips,

remembering perhaps
        their train to Augusta,
over waterways
      that lead to the Saluda;

and black men who carry their luggage
      beneath live oak branches
          with hanging, Spanish moss.

Asa Gray— his botany text in the hands
of every schoolchild—

stands that day before
            great minds of science and
reads two new papers, his plant research

that supports Darwin at a time
when *Origin of Species*
                    is still on the writing table.

To know truth
            before all others learn.

Joseph Dalton Hooker,
        Darwin's cherished confidante,
left a section of not yet published
        Origin of Species
           where his children found it

and used the leaves of paper
           to color and scribble.

On April 12, 1859,
        Darwin writes to Hooker,
I have the old MS, don't fear,
it's only a delay in publishing,

worse if I lose your wisdom
commenting on it.
Thank your wife for starting
to copy it out.

Hooker sighs, *How I wish D*
could stamp and fume at me,
instead of his good-heartedness.

Darwin doted on his own children,
           not all of whom lived long.

That day is Alfred Russel Wallace,
        the 13th in the Malayan islands,

        as he ends six months in Batchian,
to Ternate, sailing on a kora-kora government boat,
its less-than-hard-rowing crew;

and there he finds correspondence
                from Darwin
concerning their co-discovered theory
of natural selection,

a new time of science begins
in island light.

April 1859, and Frederic Church
has finished his painting *Heart of the Andes*,
                    dear tribute
to master Humboldt's cherished *Kosmos*:

Chimborazo
above the Andean peaks.

(My own copies of *Kosmos*
are the color of red maple leaves in autumn.)

Church readies the bright canvas
                    for display.
Crowds flow by month's end,
            a quarter a view for
*maximal diversity of life and landscape
the* summum bonum *of aesthetic joy.*

Search online for *Heart*, or go to New York
where it hangs.
                    You, too, might prefer no other.

That day, in Illinois,
        Stephen Douglas considers
the right of the people
of the Territories to govern themselves
in all their domestic relations—

        as he researches popular sovereignty
in colonial form, applicable
            for his moment...

        and Lincoln has business
in the Bloomington courts northeast

and hears news:
        friend Ward Hill Lamon's young wife
is dead at 33, burial in Bloomington
        on April 14, 1859.

The wild wind chanted a dirge
through the trees around the last
resting place of the departed.

Did Lincoln despair for his mother,
        young death, and the poem
that obsessed him always,
O why should the spirit of Mortal
be proud?

        Back home, with a sigh he writes a friend
I must in candor say
I do not think myself fit for the presidency,
I really think it best for our cause
that no concerted effort,
such as you suggest,
should be made.

That day, Gregor Mendel is likely
        about his famed work crossbreeding peas
in his abbey's garden.

        Which genes do I owe to James?
The "Carson sense of humor,"
highlights in my hair of Scottish red?

Wee vole, you and I share coding genomes!
                thanks to common creatures
eighty million years ago

        when this bluff was a warm
Cretaceous place
of exposed ocean rocks.

Come back,
                and I'll tell you.

That week, in spring grass of the bluff
        men stroll with muddy spades
to make a place
        for James P.,

friends and family
        shattered.

The preacher rides in on his mount.

Permelia wonders about the rest of her life,
        two small boys to raise.

Worst of times, better elsewhere.

Autumn comes, the bluff is brown and red,

while in England
the first edition of *Origin of Species*
sells out in a day.

On history's timeline: eight days
          after that publication,
John Brown is hanged.

          Origin's New York edition
comes out after Christmas,
          and Asa Gray gives his copy
to New England intellectuals
enthralled with Brown,

whose soul is marching…

3

Correlations

Might I make a great journey,
        over land and Western forests,
for a week or two …

        Might I sail on a great ship
beneath its square rig masts
and take a voyage I'd never have courage for,
        even with a native guide, £400 a year
                and a boy's ambition

even with time-traveled music along,
        electric groove,

and I'd ship home unusual life
for historic cabinets and spend weeks
        on my return naming and labeling,
my quill pen stories.

What if I had traveled with Hooker,
        ground-breaking botanist
(no pun intended)
        on his research trips?

        We'd take the road
from Temi to the Tessta
pick the berry Houttuynia,
        like strawberries;

at Doomree, we'd see
        hills of quartz and gneiss,
leaving behind the Caesulunia,
                its racemes of orange blossums;

the snows of Kinchinjunga,
        Sikkim's holiest place;

the village of Tehonpong,
where we pass groves of paper-yielding
Edgeworthia Gardneri,
            its fragrant yellow flowers.

My tent at night
was a Noah's Ark for bugs.

We'd share the Rajah's gift
of Tibet tea,
            jububes, plums and Lhassa fruit,
but what to do with that
eighty pounds of rancid yak butter
            bundled in yak-hair cloth?

Sorry, Dad, I love you
but our real voyages were hard.
          Mom and I wanted to leave you
and your Carson temper at the side
of the vacation road
          till you cheered up....

I buried my eyes in a child's biography
          of John Muir till we arrived
                    at places he defended:
the Grand Canyon, the Petrified Forest...

and some years we drove to his Colorado, too,
where once a great aspen
          of the San Juan Wilderness

had a carving in its white bark,
Kit Carson 1859,

for Kit was in that area at the time,
negotiating with the Ute Indians,

times before
          he persecuted the Navajo

and left in their tragic wake
sin worthy
of a prophet's call.

April 12, 1961,
      Yuri Gagarin's flight.
I was four,

      but not long later
my bedroom map of the solar system
was colored with current knowledge:
      Jupiter's twelve moons, Saturn's nine—
          none for Pluto.

Find the Big Dipper, said
      eagle-eyed Dad, helping me learn,
and you can find the North Star,
and now you can draw
with your eyes the Little Dipper.

Find the brightest star, then
you can draw Canis Major...
      My buddy and I tried.
Hey, that's Orion. No, it's not.
Yes, it is. You're an asshole.
          Junior scientists,
          advancing human knowledge....

      So, we mapped our own.
There's Soda Bottle, pouring
stars into the night. There's
our creek, there's a candy bar,
and there's President Kennedy...

A solar storm
in the late summer of 1859

        brightened the night
for Rocky Mountain gold miners
      who woke up as if to Christ's coming,
and New Englanders read their newspapers
     in the glow of night.
Telegraphs failed.

Volcanoes, storms
        make sharp analogies.

     For Hudson River masters,
Cotopaxi by Church was America blood red
      for the bright abyss
        of Eden destroyed,

and brush strokes of mourning fell
upon the paradise rocks.

Slavery is a moral volcano,
       preached Frederick Douglass,
a burning lake, a hell on the earth,
smoke and stench of whose torments
ascend upward forever,

      and another black preacher warned,
From the firmament of Providence
today, a meteor has fallen,
upon the volcano of American sympathies,
and though, for a while,
it may seem to sleep,

yet its igneous power
shall communicate
to the slumbering might of the volcano,

and it shall burst forth
in one general conflagration

of revolution that shall bring
about universal freedom.

Walking, I see a tree stump—
              but no, it's a veteran's stone,
Ohio infantry,
        a life cut down.

        Three days before Lincoln dies
is April 12, 1865,

the Army of Northern Virginia
        stack their arms and their furled flags,

        and Lincoln shares with his friend Lamon
about his haunting dream:
        throngs of people grieving in the White House
for the death of the president,
              killed by an assassin....

I read another grave, this one from 1882,
the year Mary Lincoln died,

and here is the grave of a man born
in 1912, the same as Dad....

April 12, 1912, and the *Titanic*
is speeding toward New York.

Another veteran's grave:
Army World War II.

In my daydreams, now it's April 12, 1945:
        Jesus Christ and Gen. Jackson!

exclaims Harry Truman that day
        when he's summoned to FDR's office,
certain that he's in trouble, which he is,
as Eleanor meets him there.
              Harry, the president is dead.

My father is on Okinawa with
the 96th Infantry Division, and

my mother is a teacher
            in a one-room schoolhouse,
loved by her students.

            To a mourning nation, Truman assures:
When I fought in France
with the 35th Division,
I saw good officers and men
fall and be replaced. I know the strain,
the mud, the misery,
the utter weariness of the soldier
in the field. And I know too
his courage, his stamina, his faith
in his comrades, his country and himself....

            April 12, 1945, a young soldier
finds human skin
            meant for lamp shades

on the autopsy table
            at Buchenwald,
liberated the day before,

            and the camp's newly freed terrorize townsfolk
who had seen the trains to the camp,
saw them leave empty,
            claimed they could not know.

I circle back to the grave of John P.,
    that hand pointing upward

now reminds me of the day
    when I walked toward Miami sea
from the Holocaust memorial:

the great hand to the silent sky,
    green bronze of anguish and
scrambling bodies on the wrist
    and on the nearby wall,
Jews' names, so many names,

if indeed you can count them,
says the Lord.

  My Orthodox friend loves so much
the paths of the great sages of the Mishnah

and all the centers of Jewish learning
    for the Balvi and Yerushalmi
through times of goyish hospitality or condemnation
    that flowed together as streams
for a *Sea of Halakhah,*

    justice and healing for the world,
faithful to The Name.

    How many of my Gentile days
would I count back to a time
    Mom and Dad and I lived on our little hill
and my world was toys, our dog,
my cars and planet map,
    Jesus and Santa,

    Eichmann… a name on TV
about whom I asked my mom.

I don't remember what she said.
What a bitter blessing to begin to know
                    such things so young,
when faith contends
                    with hardest things:

photos at which you stare,
                    a culture's tributaries
that run sick with evil,
                    blood and ash
even as children play somewhere
                    in safety.

                    As the Lord lives,
truth's arc stretches long,
                    even through Hell's burning,
and beauty is a daily gift,
                    though trust is hard.

But *do not forget the things*
that your eyes have seen nor to let them
slip from your mind
all your days

and I scribble in my drafts,
I'm sorry, I'm so sorry.

I'm sorry.

Wherever men and women
are persecuted, said Wiesel,
        once a prisoner at Buchenwald,
that place must—at that moment—
become the center of the universe.

        In daydreams I rejoin Route 51
and drive that road down south
        400 miles, through Cairo,
past Graceland, south
                till I reach Granada, Mississippi
and then turn west toward Money

        where Emmett Till
was murdered and
        tossed weighted-down
into the summer Tallahatchie.

The evil of racial injustice…
        preached Dr. King,
the crying voice of a little
Emmett Till, screaming
from the rushing waters.

Voices followed
                        toward the center,
for the sake of a just world.

Now, in my dreams,
                it's April 12, 1963, Good Friday,
and Dr. King and friend Ralph Abernathy
        are arrested by "Bull" Connor.
King soon writes
                "Letter from Birmingham Jail."

        The prophet calls:
Will the Lord be pleased

with thousands of rams,
with tens of thousands
of rivers of oil?

Shall I give my firstborn
for my transgression,
the fruit of my body
for the sin of my soul?

He has told you, O mortal,
what is good; and what
does the Lord require of you
but to do justice,
and to love kindness,
and to walk humbly
with your God?

Wishful thinking: a new call
       like one we all heard
when my friends and I were young,
       fall classes barely started,
brown bodies of the sea,

students of divinity
          with books for an afternoon
on our towels on warm sand
       down shore from war's *Corpus Christi.*

We passed around texts of justice
          like plates, sampling ideas,
and I was reading Karl Barth,
       stuck in the fine print,

       Marie had to pass Greek,
so she was reading that,
       and Sarah loved Hebrew
that favored her archaeology,

though she was off somewhere,
          holding hands with Lisa
as waves managed the shore.

I dream that the Reformers
       went to the beach,
Luther and his beer belly
          pale in the sun, Calvin
stern and systematic
       when the beach ball
          hit him on the head

       as they searched
for God's mercies among
       doctrines made and lost
          then preached for
a billion congregations.

Michele padded across
the promenade to electric groove,
                black hair long and wet
as I picture Christ's,
        earth's water dripping
from the Lord of the waters

                and blessing us as we grew brown
and read and dreamed, the sand
                        between our prayers.

4

A Parting Kiss

Here is a young man's grave, 1891,
        the year Grandma was born.

The cover of my 1891 county plat book
        back home is the color of damp oak bark,

and inside is the childish coloring
        of my mom, young and mischievous
in the 1920s and ready with her pencils
            to go to work on the cartographic leaves,
lands demarked with acreage and names
        and little Mildred's happy colors.

Hear me across the decades, Joseph Dalton Hooker:
these things do happen!

After this, I'll decorate her grave
        in town, and Dad's beside her.

There is a charming flower called
  Oconee bells,
    Shortia galacifolia,
found only in the Carolinas,
  a few other places.

Asa Gray hoped
for 38 years to find one in the wild,

as long as the lame man at Beth-zatha
    who never knew until that day
if he could be well.
  Hope takes you on long journeys.

    Oconee, Illinois, is much easier,
just up 51.
  We drove there
on the way to see Aunt Peg,
  sister of Grandma and long-ago James T.

  One year, Peg's tree was decorated
and the cookies were warm.
  I played by myself on the floor
while the grown-ups talked.
    I don't remember trying to fold a cat in half
and put it in a toy dump truck,
  but that was the story
told about me for years, so I'll stick to it.

    Darwin would agree: cats,
though cruel to mice, are wonders,
    evolved with elastic spines,
easy shoulder blades,
  the greater ability to twist and run,
to be molded into boxes, shapes….

Much later, and I was on my own

more or less, chatting with my folks
on a weekend when rates were low.
                    Dad mentioned that
Peg was dying, felt afraid.

        I wrote her a letter as best I could
about God's love, and said a prayer
                    it would give her hope.

                        So that she'd smile,
I wrote that I'd sworn off
folding cats.

The Nickel Plate Line once rushed
                   toward East St Louis
near where Dad hauled fuel
          for filling stations on old 66,

                         and in the city
               shots were fired last night,
and in many cities, little towns,
          schools shut-down, night clubs,
               children, men, and women dead,
                    incidents of lethal force,
symbols of hatred sprayed.
               I hear about them in television echo
as I get dressed and take notes.

—*The armed man should be feared*
(protect us, O Michael)

—*Wisdom cries out in the street;*
in the squares,
she raises her voice.

—*Justice is turned back,*
and righteousness stands
at a distance; for truth stumbles
in the public square.

—*Why was man created alone?*
Is it not true that the Creator
could have created the whole of humanity?
But man was created alone to teach you
that whoever kills one life
kills the world entire,
and whoever saves one life
saves the world entire.

Let us finish what we are doing,

go out, and befriend an ER doctor,
a nurse with splatter on the scrubs,

a chaplain who's seen very much,
and learn of trauma,
grief unhealed,

and then we'll go to the sanctuary
beloved by generations,

and it is filled with prayer requests
for victims of violence of all kinds,
and you can't get inside
for the number of request cards
pressing against the walnut door

and light can't pass through
the colored windows
for the cards are stacked to the rafters,
the social hall is full,
and the trustees have earmarked
funds for mercy's work.

Let us sing hopeful songs
and pray while holding
someone around the shoulder,
and since we're outside already

let us go to streets and squares,
the country places,
night and day
where wisdom calls.

Once there was a cross that stood along 51
        by the timber at the site
of Grandma's farm.

      G
      E
      T
RIGHT WITH
      G
      O
      D

On our Saturday trips,
        I looked for the cross
in hopes it would reappear
        in those Okaw bottoms,

               but it was swept by high water
to float upon the river
perhaps to warn fishermen
        for their souls.

Get right with God, for nothing but God
        is promised.
God provides, but
        much is a mystery.

How awesome is this place,
        how full of dread,
            said Jacob at Beth-el.
How awesome is *makom*, and God's name
        is *Makom*, for God *is*
the place of the world,
and the world is not his place.

Ashes unto ashes
        shaped for a likeness;

Earth is charged
          with Spirit, *nephesh*, breath of God.

The tangled bank
          and the quantum entanglement,
                    creatures and plants and stones
and the highest Heavens
          are full of Your Glory.

We know by faith,
          yet we are often downcast,
the ladder to Heaven hot to the touch,
          the ones we love are gone,

and we wait,
          lost and never good enough
                    until we're lifted after all,
urged to walk upright, believe and love.

Time to go, till next time…

Years ago
       we walked the fields,
ate blackberries from the vine
         that wound around the trunk of the willow
that grew with the blue spruce.

Goldfinch lit upon the
        of meadow foxtail, mourning dove,
always heard, invisible, gray against gray
between the glacier's ridges.

When you're out to walk,
       you want time to stretch,
a companionable hike adapted
to the sun's slow arc.

Countryside baptizes stories,
       pioneer cabins in timber boundaries,
height of prairie grass,

waters of justice and streams of memory.
       They must flow together somewhere,
and the river fills the stream.

Then as now I see the land
        through names written down,
and carved into white stone,
on old pages in cursive hand
        and hand-set print.

If I say, "Surely the darkness shall cover me,
and the light around me become night",
even the darkness is not dark to you;
the night is as bright as the day.

Little vole, by the time I write this
          you're long gone.

You and your species live a few months or so,
as if a sicky child of my ancestors' generations.
          But we're kin,
and go the way of all the earth
          and trust there's more.

Oaks of the bluff's slope
              watch the river flow,
and the combine driver
reappears from his cultivated plain,
              and we wave,
good neighbors till we pass again.

Railroads run in memory
              drivers on country crossings
look for the caboose.

Hands wring, hands fold in prayer,
              hands open,
we don't know what to do,
but reliably we reach toward things of earth
              and things of Heaven.

The days of our life are soon gone,
and we fly away,
so teach us to count our days
that we may gain a wise heart.

The day's clouds for my driving home
              are what they are,
and contrails, too:
              droplets around particles of dust,
billions in the cool upper air.

A child thinks: *God shapes clouds,*
the ice cream cone, the bunny, and the leaf.

Today, one cloud for me is a mourning dove,
              another is a gun,
another is a pair of praying hands,
              and another is a parting kiss

as the beloved goes out the door.

Notes and Acknowledgments

This sequence incorporates the following poems, in whole or in part:

"Hopewell Point," "Democratic Cookout," "Settlement": from my chapbook, *Dreaming at the Electric Hobo*, Finishing Line Press, 2015.

"Testimony," "Pumpjacks," "Young Death," "Northeast of Marytown," "Little River," "Zion's Church Road," and "State Prison: Do Not Pick Up Hitchhikers": from my chapbook, *Little River*, Finishing Line Press, 2017.

"Summer Sky," "Cemetery Caretaker": from my chapbook, *Small Corner of the Stars*, Finishing Line Press, 2017.

"Little River" and "Settlement" first appeared in *Big Muddy*.

"Land of Lincoln" first appeared in *Paddock Review*.

Notes

Part 1

["Quiet for daydreams"]: John Carroll Power, *History of the Early Settlers of Sangamon County, Illinois* (Springfield, IL: E. A. Wilson & Co., 1876), 188, records James' death and family history. There, his name is James S. Carson. His father John is buried beside him (not far from John's sister Sarah Lorton); James' mother, Margaret, is buried in Loami, Illinois; but James' wife Permelia's burial place is not known.

["Driving here, I passed"]: The end of the poem alludes to Thoreau's *Walden*, the chapter "Where I Live, and What I Lived For": "I have frequently seen a poet withdraw, having enjoyed the most valuable part of a farm, while the crusty farmer supposed that he had got a few wild apples only. Why, the owner does not know it for many years when a poet has put his farm in rhyme, the most admirable kind of invisible fence, has fairly impounded it, milked it, skimmed it, and got all the cream, and left the farmer only the skimmed milk."

["Confederation of the great Miami"]: On the native visitor, see *History of Fayette County, Illinois* (Philadelphia: Brink, McDonough & Co., 1878) 10.

["I drove here by U.S. 51"]: "The tangled bank" is a metaphor for the beauty and diversity of life, is from the poetic final paragraph of Darwin's *Origin of Species*, said to be a hill in Kent that had the force of insight of Newton's apple and Archimedes' bath, as discussed at https://www.theguardian.com/uk/2000/oct/22/booksnews.peopleinscience Accessed December 21, 2018. This poem is for Stacey Stachowicz.

["John's son was James P."]: James Starrett Carson is one of the Revolutionary War veterans buried in Fayette County, Illinois, who are commemorated on a monument at the county courthouse. The monument was unveiled on July 4, 1976. On James Starrett Carson and his history, see: http://dugamer.tripod.com/jamesstarretcarson/home.html Accessed December 12, 2018; https://www.ancestry.com/boards/thread.aspx?mv=flat&m=56&p=surnames.carson Accessed December 14, 2018.

["The air is fresh, the birds call"]: The italicized quotations are from Asa Gray, *Field, Forest, and Garden Botany: A Simple Introduction to the Common Plants of the United States East of the Mississippi, Both Wild and Cultivated*, in *Gray's School and Field Book of Botany* (New York: Ivison, Phinney, Blakeman, & Co., 1869), 335, 87, 103. Gray, Alexander von Humboldt, Charles Darwin, and Joseph Dalton Hooker were all well-known for their work in botany and biogeography.

["If I could paint in Hudson River style"]: On Church and his famous painting, see Kevin J. Avery, *Church's Great Picture: The Heart of the Andes* (New York: The Metropolitan Museum of Art, 1993). Church signed his name in the bark of a foreground tree. On Humboldt, see the note below for Section II, "May 5, 1859." On other Civil War era painters, see Eleanor Jones Harvey, *The Civil War and American Art*. (Washington, D. C.: Smithsonian American Art Museum, in association with Yale University Press, 2012) 45.

["Never spin your pistol"]: The poem alludes to an early scene in the 1993 film *Tombstone. Why, O Lord ...* is Psalm 10:1. *The Lord is your keeper...* is Psalm 121:5, 7. James T. Carson is buried in Vandalia, Illinois, beside his parents Mac and Alice Carson (my dad's grandparents).

["*L'homme armé doibt on doubter*"]: "The Armed Man" is a Renaissance tune used in many settings of the Mass. https://www.nytimes.com/2006/02/26/arts/music/arms-and-the-mass-or-why-does-this-liturgy-sound-so-familiar.html?auth=login-email&login=email Accessed January 17, 2020. The conclusion of the section alludes to the story of Elijah at Mount Horeb, 1 Kings

19; and to Lincoln's Second Inaugural Address (... "until every drop of blood drawn with the lash shall be paid by another drawn with the sword"...). Among Civil War weapons, there was actually a Sharps rifle with the patent date April 12, 1859: https://civilwartalk.com/threads/model-1859-sharps-breech-loading-rifle.90569/ Accessed December 12, 2018.

["—a sudden, gentle sound"]: The allusion is to Robert Burns' well-known poem, "To a Mouse, On Turning Her Up in Her Nest with the Plough, November 1785." The Carsons are said to have originated in Dumfriesshire, where Burns last lived and where he is buried. My vole was actually my little friend in my backyard in Ohio, but I took the artistic license of imagining wee beastie in this cemetery.

Part 2

The history behind this sequence is as follows:

• ["Coincidences of history"]: On April 11-14, 1859, John Brown makes a visit to Peterboro, NY, where he stays at the home of Gerritt Smith, one of Brown's group of supporters called "Secret Six". His speech to Smith's friend's on April 13 occasioned the praise about his Christian convictions. Brown then traveled to his farm in North Elba, NY, and then to Concord, where he gave a lecture with Emerson and Thoreau in attendance. See Zoe Trodd and John Stauffer (eds), *Meteor of War: The John Brown Story* (Maplecrest, NY: Brandywine Press, 2004), 101-102; Stephen B. Oates, *To Purge This Land with Blood: A Biography of John Brown* (New York: Harper & Row, 1970), 268-269. If I were to point out... is Edwin Morton to Franklin Stanford, April 13, 1859, quoted in Trodd and Stauffer, 102 and Oates 269. On a significant slave auction during March, 1859, see http://www.eyewitnesstohistory.com/slaveauction.htm Accessed December 13, 2018.

• ["Those who teach of time"]: On April 12, 1859, Charles and Mary Lyell are conducting geological research the mouth of the Rhine River. The italicized words are from Charles Lyell to Mrs. Bunbury, April 22, 1859, in Mrs. [Katharine M.] Lyell (ed), *Life Letters and Journals of Sir Charles Lyell, Bart*, Vol II (London: John Murray, 1881), 322-323; Leonard G. Wilson, *Lyell in America: Transatlantic Geology, 1841-1853* (Baltimore: The Johns Hopkins University Press, 1998), 64ff. Lyell, who revolutionized geology with his view of uniformitarianism and geological change over epochs of time, wrote *Principles of Geology* (1830) which in turn was a major influence upon Darwin's theories.

• ["Asa Gray—his botany text in the hands"]: On April 12, 1859, America's foremost botanist Dr. Asa Gray presents two papers to the American Academy of Arts and Sciences: "On the Genus Croomia, and Its Place in the Natural System" and "Characters of Ancistrophora, a New Genus of the Order Compositæ, Recently Detected by Charles Wright, Esq. in the Eastern Part of Cuba."See "Four Hundred and Sixty-Fourth Meeting. April 12, 1859. Monthly Meeting." *Proceedings of the American Academy of Arts and Sciences*, vol. 4, 1857, pp. 197–202. JSTOR, www.jstor.org/stable/20021233. Also A. Hunter Dupree, *Asa Gray, American Botanist, Friend of Darwin*. Baltimore, MD: Johns Hopkins University Press, 1988.

• ["Joseph Dalton Hooker"]: On April 12, 1859, Darwin writes his friend Joseph Dalton Hooker about Hooker's children, who scribbled on Hooker's copy of the *Origin* manuscript. See Darwin to J. D. Hooker, 12th [April 1859], and footnote 1. Darwin Correspondence Project, University of Cambridge, https://www.darwinproject.ac.uk/letter/?docId=letters/DCP-LETT-2453. xml;query=april%2012%201859;brand=default Accessed December 14, 2018.

• ["The day is Alfred Russel Wallace"]: On April 12 (13th in the Malayan islands), 1859. Alfred Russel Wallace, who conceived of natural selection independently of Darwin, receives a letter from Darwin, concerning their respective research on natural selection: Ross Slotten, *A Heretic in Darwin's Court: The Life of Alfred Russel Wallace* (New York: Columbia University Press) 163f, 168. Also, Alfred Russel Wallace, *The Malay Archipelago: The Land of the Orang-utan and the Bird of Paradise. A Narrative of Travel with Studies of Man and Nature*. London: Macmillan, 1869.

• ["April 1859, and Frederick Church"]: In mid-April 1859. Frederic Edwin Church was arranging the upcoming viewings for his great painting *The Heart of the Andes*, which has a private viewing on April 27, followed by a public viewing attended by 13,000 people. On Church and his painting in addition to Avery's *Church's Great Picture*, see also Stephen Jay Gould, "Church, Humboldt, and Darwin: The Tension and Harmony of Art and Science," in Franklin Kelly, with Stephen Jay Gould and James Anthony Ryan, *The Paintings of Frederic Edwin Church*. Washington: National Gallery of Art, 1989. 94-107. https://www.nga.gov/content/dam/ngaweb/research/publications/pdfs/frederic-edwin-church.pdf Accessed December 15, 2018. *maximal diversity*… is from Gould, "Church, Humboldt, and Darwin" 100. Gould discusses the contrast of Darwin with Humboldt on pages 100, 102, and 103. Church planned to ship the painting to the man who inspired it, Alexander von Humboldt, but Humboldt died (on May 5, 1859) before Church could carry out his plan.

On Humboldt and his influence on Darwin, Wallace, Thoreau, Church, John Muir, and many others, see Aaron Sachs, *The Humboldt Current: Nineteenth Century Exploration and the Roots of American Environmentalism* (New York: Penguin Books, 2006); Laura Dassow Walls, *Alexander von Humboldt and the Shaping of America* (Chicago: University of Chicago Press, 2009); and Andrea Wulf, *The Invention of Nature: Alexander von Humboldt's New World* (New York: Alfred A. Knopf, 2015). Humboldt—who although the namesake of many schools and towns is nearly forgotten today—inspired so many in his time, with his long research voyages and his comprehensive vision of the universe. I'm pleased that these poems were completed in the year of the 250th anniversary of Humboldt's birth and the 160th of his death

• ["That day, in Illinois"]: On April 11, 1859, Stephen A. Douglas writes to George Bancroft about the colonial roots of popular sovereignty, and he continues that week to research the topic for his speeches. Robert W. Johannsen (ed.), *The Letters of Stephen A. Douglas* (Urbana: University of Illinois Press, 1961), 442-443.

Meanwhile, on April 11, 1859, Lincoln is in Springfield, IL. On April 12 he is likely en route to Bloomington, IL, about 70 miles to the north; and then in April 13, he is in Bloomington. Paul M. Angle, *Lincoln 1854-1861* (Springfield, IL: The Abraham Lincoln Association, 1933), 276; Roy P Basler, et al. (eds.), *The Collected Works of Abraham Lincoln*, Vol. III (New Brunswick: Rutgers University Press, 1953) 376-377. *The wild wind...* is from the report in the Bloomington *Pantagraph*, April 20, 1859, on the burial of Angelina (Turner) Lamon, quoted in Angle 276. *I must in candor...* is from Angle 276, and from Basler 377.

• ["That day, Gregor Mendel is likely"]: Mendel conducted his research on hereditary traits in 1856-1863. On Mendel's paper discussing his research, see for instance Kiona M. Smith, "Why Everyone Overlooked Gregor Mendel's Groundbreaking Paper," Feb. 8, 2018, https://www.forbes.com/sites/kionasmith/2018/02/08/why-everyone-overlooked-gregor-mendels-groundbreaking-paper/#36c4e8667d76 Accessed December 13, 2018. On voles and humans, see "Why Mouse Matters," National Human Genome Research Institute, https://www.genome.gov/10001345/importance-of-mouse-genome/ Accessed October 26, 2018; Julianna Kettlewell, " 'Fidelity gene' found in voles," BBC News, http://news.bbc.co/uk/2/hi/science/nature/3812483.stm Accessed October 26, 2018.

• ["That week, in spring grass"]: April 12, 1859, my great-great-grandfather

James P. Carson dies when he is accidentally shot by another hunter and is buried in the Lorton Cemetery in Fayette County, Illinois.

• ["Worst of times, better elsewhere"]: On April 30, 1859, the first weekly installment of Dicken's *A Tale of Two Cities* was published in Dicken's periodical *All the Year Round*, and installments continued to November 26, 1859. My line "Worst of times, better elsewhere" is of course a paraphrase of the novel's famous opening.

For the influence of *On the Origin of Species* in the U.S., after its November, 1859 publication in London and its January, 1860 publication in New York, see Randall Fuller, *The Book That Changed America: How Darwin's Theory of Evolution Ignited a Nation* (New York: Viking Press, 2017).

Part 3

["Might I make a great journey"]: For the travels of pioneering botanist Sir Joseph Dalton Hooker, a few incidents of which I adapt here, see his *Himalayan Journals* (London: John Murray, 1855), I, 23, 293, 298-299, 312; II, 33. *My tent at night ...* is from II, 42-43.

["Sorry, Dad, I love you"]: On the tree carving *Kit Carson 1859*, see http://www.santafenewmexican.com/news/local_news/kit-carson-left-his-mark-literally/article_2d5b85d1-ad68-58d4-aad3-be81688daca2.html Accessed December 12, 2018.

["Yuri Gagarin's flight was"]: Gagarin was the first human to travel into outer space, completing one orbit on April 12, 1961. On Yuri's Night, see https://yurisnight.net/about/ Accessed December 13, 2018.

["A solar storm"]: On the 1859 solar storm, see https://www.perspectaweather.com/blog/2016/9/6/1010-am-the-super-solar-storm-of-1859-now-known-as-the-carrington-event Accessed December 13, 2018. On slavery and the metaphor of volcanos, see: Harvey, *The Civil War in American Art*, 43. *Slavery is a moral volcano...* is Frederick Douglass, "The American Apocalypse," An Address Delivered in Rochester, NY, June 16, 1861, quoted in Harvey 43. *From the firmament...* is from Rev. J. S. Martin, sermon from December 2, 1859 at Pittsburgh Wylie Street AME Church, quoted in Harvey, *The Civil War and American Art* 45.

["Walking, I see a tree stump—"]: On the stacking of the flags, and Lincoln's activity, see Brooks D Simpson, "April 12, 1865: Stacking Arms," April 12, 2015, https://cwcrossroads.wordpress.com/2015/04/12/april-12-1865-stacking-arms/ Accessed December 18, 2018. On Lincoln's dream, see: Doris Kearns Goodwin, *Team of Rivals: The Political Genius of Abraham Lincoln* (New York: Simon and Schuster, 2005), 728-729. Goodwin notes that historian Don Fehrenbacher has cast doubts on Lamon's story, but she adds that Lincoln did have what he considered portentous dreams which he then shared with others.

On Buchenwald, see: "Liberation of Buchenwald Concentration Camp," http://www.scrapbookpages.com/Buchenwald/Liberation0.html Accessed November 1, 2018. On Truman's day, see Robert F. Door, "Harry Truman's Long Day on April 12," https://www.defensemedianetwork.com/stories/harry-trumans-long-day-on-april-12-1945/ Accessed November 1, 2018

["I circle back to the grave of John P."]: On the Holocaust Memorial in Miami Beach, see http://holocaustmemorialmiamibeach.org Accessed December 18, 2018. *If indeed...* is Genesis 15:5, *Do not forget...* is Deuteronomy 4:9. I deeply appreciate the friendship of Maharat Rori Picker Neiss, who inspired a portion of this poem. Amidst her busy schedule she read the poem and, later, the whole manuscript.

[*"Wherever men and women"*]: The entire quotation is, "Wherever men and women are persecuted because of their race, religion, or political views, that place must – at that moment – become the center of the universe." Elie Wiesel, Nobel Prize Speech, The Elie Wiesel Foundation for Humanity, http://eliewieselfoundation.org/elie-wiesel/nobelprizespeech/ Accessed December 14, 2018. *The evil of racial injustice...* is from a quotation in "Emmett Till's Death Inspired a Movement," https://nmaahc.si.edu/blog-post/emmett-tills-death-inspired-movement. Accessed December 14, 2018. *Will the Lord be pleased....* is Micah 6:7-8.

Part 4

["Here is a young man's grave, 1891"]: *The Platbook of Fayette County, Illinois* was compiled and published by Alden, Ogle & Co., 1891. http://www.historicmapworks.com/Atlas/US/10447/Fayette+County+1891/ Accessed January 14, 2019.

["The charming Oconee bells"]: On Asa Gray's fascination with and search for the Oconee bells, see "Shortia galacifolia: A Plant Rediscovered," Harvard University Herbaria & Libraries, http://botlib.huh.harvard.edu/libraries/Gray_Bicent/shortia_galacifolia.html Accessed December 14, 2018. The story of the lame man at Beth-zatha is told in John 5:2-9.

["The Nickel Plate Line once rushed"]: *Wisdom cries out…*is from Proverbs 1:20. *Justice is turned back…* is from Isaiah 59:14. *Why was man created alone? …*is a paraphrase of Talmud teachings, quoted in Gideon Frieder, "To Save the World Entire," United States Holocaust Memorial Museum, https://www.ushmm.org/remember/office-of-survivor-affairs/memory-project/featured-writers/to-save-the-world-entire Accessed December 14, 2018. The Talmud passage is Mishnah Sanhedrin 4:5. The Qur'an teaches a similar principle, in Surah 5:32.

["Once there was a cross "]: *How awesome is this place* is from Genesis 28:17. On *makom*, see Rabbi Ari Kahn, "The Place-Hamakom," http://www.aish.com/tp/i/moha/70912247.html Accessed November 16, 2018. As I said above, "the tangled bank" is a metaphor for the beauty and diversity of life, is from the poetic final paragraph of Darwin's *Origin of Species*. "Quantum entanglement" is (in quantum physics) when particles like photons interact and affect each other, although separated by considerable distances.

["Time to go, till next time…"]: *If I say…* is from Psalm 139:11-12. *[I] go the way of all the earth* is from 1 Kings 2:2.

["Oaks of the bluff's slope"]: *The days of our life are soon gone…* is from Psalm 90:10, 12.

Many thanks to Dr. Tom Dukes, who encouraged this and previous projects and who made possible my dreams of writing poetry. Many thanks also to Maharat Rori Picker Neiss, Dr. Andrea Scarpino, Dr. Steph Schroeder, Dr. Kim Kleinman, Rev. Bonnie Smith, Jane Ellen Ibur, Heather Derr-Smith, Sage Goliday, Erin Quick, the Webster Groves Starbucks, the Novel Neighbor Bookstore, the St. Louis Poetry Center, Leah Maines and the staff of Finishing Line Press, and my dear friend Stacey Stachowicz and her family.

When I was in high school in the 1970s and interested in genealogy, my great-uncle Roy Carson (1912-1984) gave me photocopies of pages from the Sangamon County, IL histories, and thus I first learned of my Carson forbearers and soon made my first visit to the Lorton Cemetery.

My love is always for my family, Beth and Emily, and our flexible cats.

Paul Stroble teaches philosophy and religious studies at Webster University in St. Louis and is also adjunct faculty at Eden Theological Seminary. A native of Vandalia, Illinois, he lives in St. Louis. A grantee of the National Endowment for the Humanities and the Louisville Institute, he has written several books, primarily church related, and numerous articles, essays, and curricular materials. Finishing Line Press has published four of his chapbooks, *Dreaming at the Electric Hobo* (2015), *Little River* (2017), *Small Corner of the Stars* (2017), and *Backyard Darwin* (2019).

www.ingramcontent.com/pod-product-compliance
Lightning Source LLC
Chambersburg PA
CBHW021159090426
42740CB00008B/1153